Adobe Photoshop Elements 2022

ILLUSTRATED GUIDE

Adobe Photoshop Elements 2022
ILLUSTRATED GUIDE

Upgrade Your Image Editing

Skills Using the Newly Released

Photoshop Elements 2022

Kent Peterson

Adobe Photoshop Elements 2022 Illustrated Guide

Copyright © 2022 by Kent Peterson

OTHER BOOKS BY THE AUTHOR

iPhone 13 Pro Max User Guide

A Complete User Guide for Beginners and Seniors to Master the New iPhone 13 Pro Max with Tips and Tricks to Use iOS 15

SCAN QR CODE TO ORDER

AVAILABLE NOW ON amazon

https://www.amazon.com/dp/B09PP7XL44

Digital Minimalism for a Productive Life

Practical Guide on How to Declutter your Digital Lives and Break Free from Social Medial Addiction

SCAN QR CODE TO ORDER

AVAILABLE NOW ON amazon

https://www.amazon.com/dp/B09J7CDXX8

Cybersecurity, Cyberwar and Cyberweapon

A Beginner's Guide to Understanding Cyber Security and How It Affects You

SCAN QR CODE TO ORDER

AVAILABLE NOW ON amazon

https://www.amazon.co.uk/dp/B09DN1926V

Contents

"I want to say a big thank you for purchasing and reading my book. I am extremely grateful and hope you found value in reading it. Please consider sharing it with friends or family and leaving a review online. Your feedback and support are always appreciated, and allow me to continue doing what I love.

Please go to

https://rebrand.ly/49ec81

or scan the QR Code

if you'd like to leave a review.

As a thank you for buying my book, I want to offer you a free eBook on How you can clear junk files from your PC and other devices.

SCAN QR CODE
OR GO TO
LINK BELOW
TO RECEIVE

https://mailchi.mp/9405d1ea2bc7/how-to-clear-junk-files-on-your-pc-and-device

Within this eBook you will learn with illustrations how you can easily clear up junk and unwanted files, so you can enjoy and fully maximize your device.

Introduction

The new Photoshop Elements 2022 can help you improve your images and make them appear spectacular, whether you're shooting enjoyable family photos or catching incredible images on film. It has been updated with a number of essential features, including new Guided Edits, which allow you to quickly make your work more dynamic-looking, Automated editing, create and share, and organization.

While you get the most out of your camera when shooting the photo, it's a whole lot simpler to obtain the editing effects you desire. However, these recent enhancements make editing a lot easier. Starting with Photoshop Elements 2022, we'll delve into all of the new features, including other things to learn about the new Photoshop Elements.

Chapter 1

Features of Adobe Photoshop Elements 2022

The features are broken down into the following:

- Automated Editing
- Guided Edits
- Create & Share
- Organization

Automated Editing

It's just a few clicks away from seeing your greatest photographs. So you can concentrate on bringing your idea to life, Adobe Sensei AI technology and automated choices perform the hard work for you.

Instantly turn images into art

Transform your photographs with effects inspired by well-known works of art or popular art styles with just one click. Apply an effect to your whole picture or just a portion of it.

Make not-so-still images

Create animated frames with moving overlays like snowflakes and glitter. Then save your images as MP4s to distribute on social media and other platforms.

Warp photos to suit any shape

Wrap a picture around an item, such as a coffee cup, or fit it within contours, such as the lenses of your subject's sunglasses, to put one shot inside another.

Make your photos more dynamic by adding motion

Transform your favorite images into moving photos with just one click—fun animated MP4s and GIFs with 2D and 3D camera movements. It's simple to do and ideal for posting on social media.

Fine-tune face tilt

By automatically altering the location of a person's face, you can ensure that everyone in your shot is looking in the appropriate direction. It's ideal for taking selfies.

Make changes to your face features

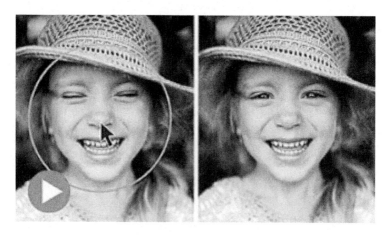

Automatically open closed eyelids, flip frowns upside down, and more to get the ideal photo every time.

Make skin smooth automatically

Ensure that everyone looks their best at all times. Skin texture may be easily softened without seeming unnatural.

Colorize images automatically

With automated colorization, you may breathe new life into old black-and-whites or adjust the hues in your photos.

Subject selection with a single click

With a simple click, you may choose the topic of your picture automatically. Then make discrete modifications to the topic or backdrop with ease.

Interesting effects and filters

Choose from five Smart Looks, which apply effects to your images automatically depending on the topic, color, and lighting. Alternatively, use your own filter and fine-tune from there.

Lessen camera shake

Everyone experiences camera shaking. Shake Reduction, thankfully, removes the blur fast, effortlessly, and automatically.

Guided Effects

Perfect photographs are just a few steps away. With 60 Guided Edits, you can easily create simple modifications, creative masterpieces, and anything in between.

Make perfect pet photos

Make your canine companions look their best. In just a few easy steps, you can frame them perfectly, change color and lighting, choose and enhance hair, repair pet-eye, and remove collars and leashes.

Increase the size of the image backgrounds

By expanding your photo's backdrop, you may simply create a gorgeous landscape or reposition your subject for the ideal social post. It's all possible thanks to Content-Aware Fill's magic.

Make your landscapes perfect

To create magnificent outdoor landscapes, just alter sky, eliminate haze, and delete undesirable items. You'll always be able to take the ideal adventure shot.

Make contemporary duotones

Using this easy Guided Edit, apply interesting, original duotone effects to your images for a lovely two-color masterpiece. Add a gradient, choose from unique preset social sizes, and more.

Scale and move objects

It's simpler than ever to choose an item, duplicate it, and alter its location, size, and more with step-by-step guidance, so you can make your creation seem exactly way you want it to.

Remove distractions easily

Remove people in the background, power wires, and other distracting elements to concentrate on your topic.

Colorize your black-and-white photos

To create a dramatic impact, highlight a particular hue or a specific item, then convert the remainder to black-and-white.

Change backgrounds quickly and easily

To make your shot even more spectacular, choose the topic of the photo and position it on a different backdrop.

Include unique patterns

Brush on a whimsical design, such as hearts or stars, to add a little something special to any shot.

Make a text using many photos

Create a visual text with a distinct picture for each letter. Make great-looking names or other words by easily adjusting and resizing your images.

Create interesting double exposures

With a stunning double exposure effect, combine two photographs into one piece of art.

Add style with borders and text

Add unique borders and text to remarkable photographs to make them stand out.

Create and Share

Begin by going to the home screen

With the useful Home page, you can get right to work and discover what's new in the product.

Experiment with different new slideshow styles

With new dynamic slideshow designs in a variety of eye-catching styles, you can show off your photographs and videos while also telling your tales.

Quote Graphics to Inspire

With pre-set themes, loads of customization, and fantastic animation choices, you can add inspiring quotations or customized inscriptions to your photos. Save your videos as MP4s so you can easily share them on Instagram and other social media platforms.

Exclusively for you—Auto Creations

Beautiful slideshows, collages, and effects are added to your photographs automatically and provided right after startup.

Built-in gifts and prints service
(Only available in the United States)

With the FUJIFILM Prints and Gifts service within Photoshop Elements, you can create and buy gallery-quality wall art, on-trend accessories, and more to display your work in style.

Stunning photo collages

With only a few clicks, you can create collages from a variety of beautiful designs. Replace backgrounds and pan and zoom photographs in your collages.

Effortless Organization

The fourth new addition in Adobe Photoshop Elements 2022 is Effortless Organization and this is what is included in it:

Automatically organize

From hundreds of hidden files to a visible representation of your images arranged by date, topic, people, locations, and events. Furthermore, your catalog structure is automatically backed up for simple recovery, allowing you to operate without stress.

NEW

In the Organizer, you can now watch GIFs. Now that the Organizer enables playback, just click to activate your GIFs.

Auto tagging helps you find images quicker

Smart Tags are applied to your images based on topics such as sunsets and birthdays, and the individuals in your photos are identified so that they may be tagged and found later.

Locate your best images with Auto Curate

Your images are automatically filtered based on quality, faces, topics, Smart Tags, and other factors, so you don't have to look for them.

System Requirements to Run Adobe Photoshop Elements 2022

The following is a list of system requirements for running Adobe Photoshop Elements 2022 at its best.

For Windows:

- Intel 6th Generation or newer processors with SSE4.1 capability, or AMD equivalent
- Microsoft Windows 10 version 2004 or later (version 21H1 is preferred); 64-bit only; Windows 7, Windows 8.1 are not supported.
- Only Windows 10 version 1903 or later supports HEIF/HEVC import. For further information, go to www.adobe.com/go/preheifinfo.
- Memory: 8 GB
- 7.2 GB of accessible hard-disk space for program installation; 3 GB for optional content download; extra free space needed for installation (cannot install on a volume that uses a case-sensitive file system or on removable flash storage devices)
- Display resolution of 1280x800 pixels (at 100 percent scale factor)
- Display driver for Microsoft DirectX 12
- A DVD-ROM player (for installation from DVD)

- For product activation and content download, you'll need an internet connection.

For macOS:

- Processor Intel 6th Generation or newer
- Mac OS X 10.15 or 10.11
- Memory: 8 GB
- 7GB of free hard drive space is needed to install software; an extra 3GB is required to download all optional material; additional free disk space is required during installation (cannot install on a volume that uses a case-sensitive file system or on removable flash storage devices)
- Display resolution of 1280x800 pixels (at 100 percent scale factor)
- A DVD-ROM player (for installation from DVD)
- For product activation and content download, you'll need an internet connection.

Chapter 2

Home Screen

Overview of Photoshop Elements' Home Screen

Congratulations on purchasing the new Adobe Photoshop Elements 2022. After you've opened Photoshop Elements 2022, you'll see the Home Screen. This screen replaces the Welcome Screen in previous versions of Photoshop Elements. In Photoshop Elements, the Home Screen displays auto-generated picture and video collages and slideshows based on imported material. It also allows you to locate new editing projects, obtain creative ideas, switch between workspaces, access recent files, and seek assistance.

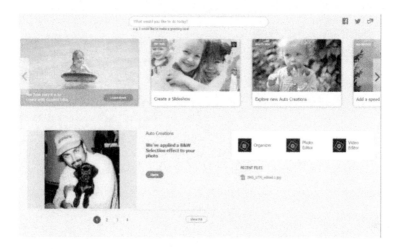

In Photoshop Elements, the Search bar at the top of the Home Screen allows you to look for help files and tutorials. To search, type the relevant text into the Search field and then hit the **"Enter"** key on your keyboard. The Home Screen displays matching results as thumbnails and hyperlinks. To view the help documentation, open the page in your web browser by clicking a thumbnail or hyperlink. Click the **"Home"** link in the breadcrumbs area in the upper-left corner of the screen to return to the Home Screen.

In Photoshop Elements, the card carousel in the top right corner of the Home Screen allows you access to new features, projects, and ideas. Click the arrows on the left and right edges of the carousel to navigate through it. New Photoshop Elements features are shown on cards titled **"What's New"** (with a blue tag). To get to them, mouse over a **"What's New"** card and click the **"Open Link"** icon to open it in your web browser. Cards with an orange tag labeled "Inspiration" reveal resources and examples of how others have used various features.

Click the **"View"** button that appears after hovering over a **"Inspiration"** card to access these resources. The "Try This" cards (marked with green tags) allow you to experiment with useful features. To test a feature, mouse over the feature card and click the **"Try"** button that appears. After that, Photoshop Elements launches and leads you through the processes with an on-screen instruction.

The program generates Auto Creations on a regular basis depending on the supplied material. In this section, you may see auto-generated picture collages, slideshows, video collages, and Candid Moments. Click the **"Open"** button next to a shown auto creation to open it. Click the "View All" button underneath the Auto Creations thumbnail to see all of the available creations. Click the number icons below the Auto Creations image to pick particular creations.

Photoshop Elements' Home Screen also includes access to the many workspaces available in the program. The Organizer window is opened by clicking the **"Organizer"** button on the Home Screen. To keep your image collection as efficient and structured as possible, use the Organizer to import, browse, and arrange photographs.

The **"Photo Editor"** window is opened by clicking the **"Photo Editor"** button on the Home Screen. This window has all of the tools for both producing and modifying photos. Users using Adobe Photoshop Elements Premiere may launch the application's video editor window by clicking the **"Video Editor"** button.

You may also open recently-accessed project files from the Home Screen in Photoshop Elements. On the Home Screen, Elements shows up to six project files in the **"Recent Files"** tab. To open one of these files fast, click its link.

In Photoshop Elements, click the **"Dismiss"** button in the upper-right corner of the window to close The Home Screen. Click the **"Home Screen"** button in the Taskbar at the bottom of the Organizer or Photo Editor windows, or re-launch the Elements program if it is closed, to return to the Home Screen.

Photoshop Elements' Home Screen: Instructions

1. When you first launch Photoshop Elements 2022, the Home Screen displays.

2. In Photoshop Elements, type the relevant word into the Search box at the top of the Home Screen to obtain support documentation.

3. Then, on your keyboard, hit the **"Enter"** key to see thumbnails and hyperlinks for related assistance files.

4. Then, to access it in your web browser, click a thumbnail or a hyperlink.

5. To access **"What's New"** features, hover over a **"What's New"** card at the top of the Home Screen and click the **"Open"** link that appears.

6. Click the **"View"** button that displays when you hover over an **"Inspiration"** card to discover inspiring ideas.

7. Click the **"Test"** button that appears when you hover over a **"Try This"** card to try a function with an on-screen instruction.

8. To open an auto creation that has been presented, click the **"Open"** button that appears next to it.

9. Click the **"View All"** button underneath the Auto Creations thumbnail to see all of the possible creations.

10. Click the number icons underneath the Auto Creations image to pick individual creations.

11. On the Home Screen, click the **"Organizer"** button to launch the **"Organizer"** window.

12. From the Home Screen, click the **"Photo Editor"** button to launch the **"Photo Editor"** window.

13. Click the link to the file that shows on the Home Screen to rapidly open recently-accessed files.

14. In Photoshop Elements, click the **"Dismiss"** button in the upper-right corner of the screen to close the Home Screen.

15. To access the Home Screen, click the **"Home Screen"** button on the Taskbar at the bottom of the Organizer or Editor, or reopen the Elements program if it has been closed.

Chapter 3

How to Open Files

Working in Photoshop Elements' Edit workspace provides you a variety of options for working with your files. You may choose file types, file sizes, and resolution when opening, saving, and exporting files. Camera raw files may also be processed and saved. These tools make it simple to integrate and optimize files of various sorts in Adobe Photoshop Elements.

You may create a blank file, open a previously used file, define which file formats to open in Photoshop Elements, and more in the Edit workspace.

The Guided Edit function is another alternative for working in the Edit workspace. When you're unclear about a process or how to complete a job, Guided Edits may aid. They enable users to accomplish complicated editing processes in a few simple steps.

How to Open Images

Instructions for using Photoshop Elements to open images

1. From the Menu Bar, choose **"File | Access . . ."** to open the **"Open"** dialog box in Photoshop Elements.

2. Go to the folder where you want to hunt for picture files in your computer's file system.

3. To open an image file in Elements, double-click it.

4. Alternatively, you may select it by clicking it once.

5. To open the dialog box, click the **"Open"** button in the lower-right corner.

6. From the Menu Bar, choose **"File | Access Recently Edited File"** to open a recently opened picture file.

7. In the side menu that opens, click the name of the previously opened picture file to re-open it.

8. Alternatively, locate the **"Open"** button at the left end of the Shortcuts Bar to open a recently opened picture file.

9. Then, to the right of the **"Open"** button, click the little downward-pointing arrow.

10. Then, from the list that displays, choose a recently opened picture.

How to Make a New Blank Document

If you want to make a site graphic, a banner, or a corporate logo and letterhead, you'll need to start from scratch.

1. Select **File > New > Blank File** from the File menu.

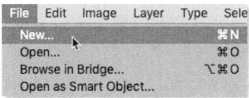

2. Select the new image's parameters and click OK.

- **Name**

  The new picture file is given a name.

- **Preset**

  Allows you to customize the width, height, and quality of photos that you want to print or display on screen. To utilize the size and resolution of data transferred to the clipboard, choose Clipboard. You can also use any open picture's size and quality to create a new image by selecting its name from the Preset menu's bottom.

- **Size**

  Choose from a list of standard sizes for the preset you've chosen.

- **Dimensions (width, height, and resolution)**

  Individually configures these parameters. Unless you've transferred data to the clipboard, the default settings are based on the last picture you made.

- **Color Mode**

  Sets the color mode of an image to RGB, grayscale, or bitmap (1 bit mode).

- **Background Contents**

  Sets the picture Background layer's color. The default color is white. To utilize the current backdrop color, choose Background Color (shown in the toolbox). Choose Translucent to make the default layer transparent and without color values; the new picture will have a Layer 1 instead of a Background layer.

Chapter 4

How to Open
a PDF Document

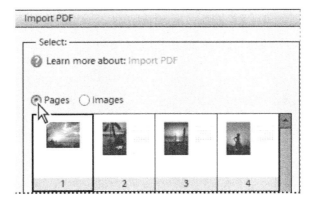

The Portable Document Format (PDF) is a flexible file format that may incorporate electronic document search and navigation functions and can represent both vector and bitmap data.

You may preview the pages and pictures in a multipage PDF file in the Import PDF dialog box before deciding whether or not to open it in the Photoshop Editor. You may either import whole pages from a PDF file (containing text and graphics) or simply the photos from a PDF file. The quality, size, and color mode of the photographs are not affected if you merely import the images. You may modify the resolution and color mode while importing pages.

> **NB:** *Each page is represented with a thumbnail image. Choose an item from the Thumbnail Size menu to increase the size.*

1. Select **File > Open** from the File menu.
2. Select **Open** after selecting a PDF file. Select an item from the Files Of Type menu to alter which file types are shown.
3. In the Import PDF dialog box, choose the **Photos option** from the Select area to import just the images from a PDF file. Choose the image(s) you wish to open. (Hold Ctrl (Windows) or Command (Mac OS) when clicking each picture to pick several photos.)
4. Select the Pages option from the Select area in the Import PDF dialog box to import pages from a PDF file, and then perform one of the following:

- If the file has many pages, click OK after selecting the page or pages you wish to open. (Press Ctrl (Windows) or Command (Mac OS) and click each page to choose several pages.)

- Accept the current name in Page Options, or input a new filename in the Name field.

- Define the width and height of the image. To prevent visual distortion due to size changes, enable Constrain Proportions.

- Accept the default (300 ppi) or input a different value for Resolution. A larger file size is associated with a greater resolution.

- Select a mode from the Mode menu (RGB to keep the photos in color, or Grayscale to automatically make them black and white). You may choose an ICC (International Color Consortium) profile from the menu if the file has one contained.

5. To conceal any error warnings throughout the import process, choose Suppress Warnings.

6. To open the file, click OK.

Adobe Photoshop Elements Workspace Basics

Here are the various Adobe Photoshop Elements Workspace Basics:

Quick

Allows you to edit photographs in Quick mode. Use this mode to perform fast and easy modifications to your picture, such as adjusting the exposure, color, sharpness, and other characteristics.

Guided

Allows you to use the Guided mode to edit photographs.

The Guided mode is a wizard-like interface that lets you create predetermined effects. When you hover the mouse cursor over a guided edit, an image appears that shows the applied effect.

Expert

Allows you to use the Expert mode to edit images.

Expert mode includes tools for fixing color issues, creating special effects, and enhancing photographs. The Quick mode includes basic color and lighting correction tools, as well as instructions for swiftly resolving common issues like red eye. Basic picture adjustments, guided activities, and photographic effects are all available in the Guided mode.

If you're new to digital photography, the Quick or Guided modes are a fantastic place to start.

If you've ever used image-editing software, you'll know that the Expert mode offers a versatile and powerful image-correction environment. It offers tools for repairing picture faults, creating selections, adding text, and painting on your photographs, as well as lighting and color-correction instructions. The Expert workspace may be rearranged to meet your specific requirements. In the Panel Bin, you may move, conceal, and reveal panels, as well as organize them. You can also zoom in and out of the picture, move the document window around, and create several windows and views.

- Active tab
- Inactive tab
- Active image area
- The Options Menu
- Photo bin / Tool Options bar
- Taskbar
- Panel bar

The menu bar

There are options for doing chores. The menus are divided into categories. The Enhance menu, for example, includes instructions for making alterations to a picture.

Mode Selector

There are buttons here to switch between the three editing modes. The Open (recently used files) and Create (photo projects) drop-downs are also available.

Toolbox

This folder contains picture editing tools.

Panel Bin

Features, activities, or controls that are logically organized.

Tools / Photo Bin

Toggles between Photo Bin and Tools Options (show and manage thumbnails of presently used photographs) (displays and sets options for the currently selected tool).

Taskbar

The most often used activities are shown as buttons for fast and simple access.

How to Customize Workspace

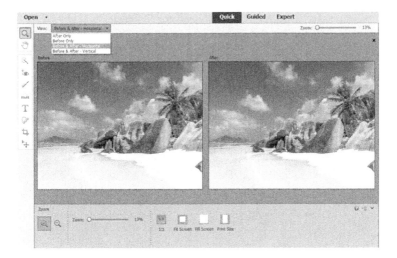

To fit your requirements, you may conceal or expose various portions of the workplace.

Toggle the corresponding icons at the bottom of the screen to conceal or display the picture bin or the Tool Options.

Use Quick mode and then one of the View settings to work split-screen with the original picture on one side and the altered photo on the other.

Chapter 5

About Toolbox

In both Quick and Expert modes, Photoshop Elements includes a toolbox to assist you in working with your photographs. The tools in the toolbox may be used to pick, enhance, sketch, and view pictures.

Toolbox in Quick Mode

In Quick mode, the toolbox offers a minimal collection of simple tools. Zoom, Hand, Quick Selection, Eye, Whiten Teeth, Straighten, Type, Spot Healing Brush, Crop, and Move are the tools accessible in this mode.

Toolbox in Expert Mode

The toolbox in Expert mode is more extensive than the toolbox in Quick mode. The following logical groupings are used to arrange the tools:

- View
- Select
- Enhance
- Draw
- Modify

Tools in the Expert mode toolbox's View group.

Tool to zoom in and out (Z)

Your picture is zoomed in or out. Zoom In and Zoom Out are related tools in the Tool Options bar.

Hand tool (H)

The picture is moved about in the Photoshop Elements workspace. This tool allows you to drag your picture.

Tools in the Expert Mode Toolbox's Select Group

Move tool (V)

Moves layers or selections.

Rectangular Marquee tool (M)

In a rectangle box, choose a portion of your picture. To make the selection a square, hold down the Shift key.

Elliptical Marquee tool (M)

Of an oval shape, choose a region in your photograph. To make the selection a circle, hold down the Shift key.

Lasso Tool (L)

In a free-form shape, choose a region in your picture.

Magnetic lasso tool (L)

Selects the high-contrast edges surrounding a shape to choose a portion of a picture.

Polygons Lasso Tool (L)

Draws straight-edged selection border segments.

Quick Selection Tool (A)

When you click or click-drag the region you wish to pick, it makes a selection based on color and texture similarities.

Brush tool for selection (A)

Selects the region where the brush will be used to paint.

Magic Wand tool (A)

In a single click, selects pixels with comparable hues.

Brush tool to refine selection (A)

By automatically recognizing the boundaries, it adds and eliminates portions from a selection.

Tool for Automatic Selection (A)

When you draw a shape around the item you wish to choose, it automatically selects it.

Tools in the Expert Mode Toolbox's Enhance Group

Eye Tool (Y)

Removes the red eye, pet eye, and closed eye effects from your photographs.

Spot Healing Brush Tool (J)

Removes blemishes from your photographs.

Healing Brush tool (J)

Removes blemishes from your picture by using a portion of it as a reference point.

Smart Brush tool (F)

Tones and colors are adjusted in particular parts of a picture.

Smart Brush tool for fine detail (F)

As if it were a painting tool, it applies the correction to specified regions of a picture.

Clone Stamp Tool (S)

You can utilize an image sample to replicate things, eliminate picture flaws, or paint over objects in your photo. You may also clone a section of one picture to another.

Tool for stamping patterns (S)

Paints with a pattern that you specify, another picture, or a pre-defined pattern.

Blur Tool (R)

Reduces details in a picture to soften rough edges or places.

Sharpen Tool (R)

Sharpens a picture by concentrating on the photo's soft edges to improve clarity and focus.

Smudge Tool (R)

Drags a finger through wet paint to simulate the activities. Color is picked up where the stroke starts and pushed in the direction you drag.

Sponge Tool (O)

Changes an area's color saturation.

Dodge Tool (O)

Enhances the brightness of certain regions of a picture. The tool may be used to bring out details in shadows.

Burn Tool (O)

The picture is darkened in certain spots. The tool may be used to emphasize details in highlights.

Tools in the Expert Mode Toolbox's Draw Group

Using the brush tool (B)

Color strokes might be gentle or harsh. It may be used to mimic airbrushing methods.

Brush tool for Impressionists (B)

Changes the colors and details in your picture to make it seem as though it was painted with stylized brush strokes.

Tool for replacing colors (B)

Replaces certain colors in your picture with ease.

Tool for erasing (E)

As you drag across the pixels in the picture, they get erased.

Background Eraser tool (E)

Allows you to effortlessly separate an item from its backdrop by converting color pixels to transparent pixels.

Magic Eraser Tool (E)

When you drag inside a picture, it changes all related pixels.

Paint Bucket Tool (K)

Fills an area with a color value that is comparable to the pixels you clicked.

Pattern Tool (K)

Instead of utilizing one of the brush tools, apply a fill or a pattern to your picture.

Gradient Tool (G)

Fills in a section of a picture with a gradient.

Color Picker Tool (I)

To create a new foreground or background color, copy or sample the color of an area in your picture.

Tool to Create Custom Shapes (U)

You may draw a variety of shapes using this tool. These forms are available in the Tool Options bar when you pick the Custom Shape tool.

The Tool Options menu also has the following shape-related tools:

- Rectangle
- Rectangle with a rounded edge
- Ellipse
- Polygon
- Star
- Line
- Selection

Type Tool (T)

Text is created and edited on your picture.

The Tool Options tab also has the following type-related tools:

- Vertical Design
- Vertical Type Mask
- Horizontal Type Mask
- Shape Text
- Selection Text

- Custom Path Text

Tool for drawing with a pencil (Pencil Tool) (N)

Creates freehand lines with a strong edge.

Chapter 6

How to Make Use of a Tool

In order to utilize a tool in Quick or Expert mode, you must first choose it from the toolbox. Then, to complete your work, utilize the numerous choices in the Tool Options bar.

Choose a tool

Choose one of the following options:

- Choose a tool from the toolbox.
- Press the tool's keyboard shortcut. To pick the Brush tool, for example, press B. In the tool tip, the keyboard shortcut for a tool is provided.

From the Tool Options bar, choose options:

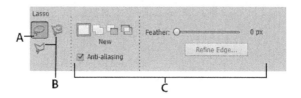

In the Photoshop Elements window, the Tool Options bar is located at the bottom. It shows the possibilities for a certain tool. In the Tool Possibilities bar, for example, if you pick the Crop tool from the toolbox, you'll see related tools (Cookie Cutter tool and Perspective Crop tool) as well as other options.

How to Undo and Redo

When working on a picture in Adobe Photoshop, you'll almost certainly need to undo anything you've done. Knowing how to go back and undo is crucial, whether you've made a mistake, changed your mind, or just need to fine-tune improvements you've previously done.

Undoing changes in Photoshop may seem straightforward on the surface, but there are a variety of techniques to undo, go back, and update changes you've made to your picture. Today, we'll look at the many undo options in Photoshop, as well as how to plan ahead while editing to make reversing simpler.

Control/Command + Z (Edit and Undo)

Selecting Undo from the Edit Menu is the easiest and most apparent method to undo changes you've made to a project in Photoshop. Undo is the first option in the Edit Menu, and utilizing the keyboard shortcut Command-Z (Mac) or Control-Z (Windows) makes it much simpler and more efficient (Windows).

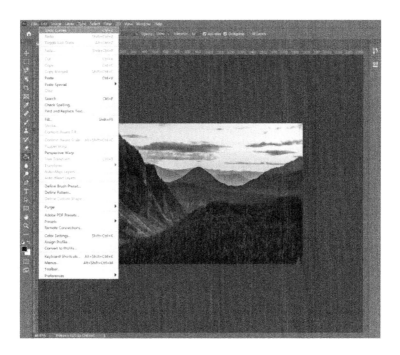

This should be the only keyboard shortcut you ever learn in Photoshop. It's fast and simple, and you'll find yourself using it again and again. Going to the Edit Menu to undo can significantly slow down your productivity. Being able to fast undo with Control/Command + Z, especially when using tools like the Clone Stamp or Healing Brush, can save you a lot of time.

Because this is very typical across most major software products, you'll likely know both the keyboard shortcut and the location inside the Edit Menu. Continuing to pick Undo (or continually pressing Command/Control + Z) in most modern software applications will enable you to walk back through the modifications you've made to your document.

You may also redo your previous undo in the Edit Menu, or use the keyboard shortcut Shift + Control + Z (Windows) or Shift + Command + Z (Mac) (Mac). The "Toggle Last State" feature in Photoshop enables you to rapidly assess the impact of the most recent modification you made on the overall picture. While you could do this by switching between Undo and Redo, if you're using keyboard short-cuts, Control + Alt + Z (Windows) or Command + Option + Z (Mac) is a somewhat faster way of turning on and off your previous edit.

Undo Shortcuts

If you've used Photoshop for a long time, you're probably aware that the Undo command used to work differently than it does today. In the current version of Photoshop, step backward works similarly to undo.

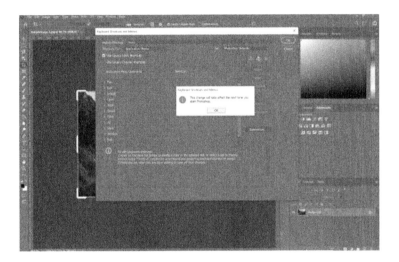

Undo capabilities that photographers use regularly in Photoshop include the ability to undo multiple changes (or move backward through the history states) and the option to turn the most recent modification on and off. The initial choice on how the undo command would work was a contentious one among Adobe developers, with the toggle function eventually winning out. However, given that practically every other current software product has an undo feature that enables users to go back in time several times, Adobe's choice to change the functionality to suit modern standards makes logical.

You may configure your options to utilize the "Legacy Undo Mode" if you prefer the old undo capabilities, either because it is what you are accustomed to or because it makes sense in your workflow.

Go to the **Edit Menu** to enable legacy undo capability. Select Keyboard Shortcuts and then "Use Legacy Undo Short-cuts" in the dialog box. After that, you'll have to restart Photoshop. When traditional undo shortcuts are enabled, pressing Command/Control + Z toggles the last change you made on and off, and pressing Alt + Control + Z (Windows) or Command + Option + Z (Mac) Steps Backward (though the history states).

Chapter 7

The History Panel

Control/Command + Z (or choosing Undo from the Edit menu) will instantly undo the previous modification or two you made to your picture in Photoshop. However, you should use the History Panel if you need to make changes that go back more than a few stages. Select History from the Window Menu to open the History Panel. This panel is quite easy in terms of Photoshop panels. It keeps track of the many stages of your document's history, as well as the modifications you've made to it.

The modifications you make to your picture will display in the history, and you can simply click back on any alteration to go back to that point in time. While the undo feature might potentially achieve this, if you need to undo a large number of changes, you can do it with a single click on the **History Panel.**

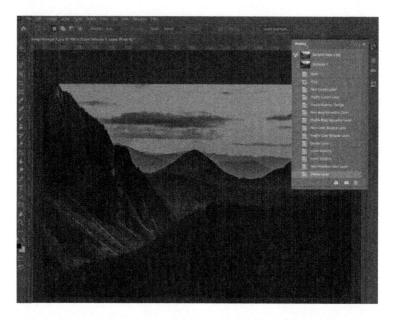

The History Panel, however, is more than simply a convenient method to undo many times; it also has several extra features. You may configure the history state for your History Brush (see below) and take point-in-time snapshots of your picture in this window. The camera icon in the lower right corner of the History Panel takes a photo of your image when you choose it. A snapshot is essentially a bookmark of a certain time in your image's history. Snapshots show at the top of the History Panel, and selecting one takes the document back to that particular moment in time.

Taking screenshots before making multi-step adjustments to your picture allows you to undo quickly if you don't like the outcome. It's also a quick method to compare and assess your picture adjustments by taking many snapshots and clicking between them.

The Historical Panel records 50 history states by default. This may seem like a lot, but each click or brush stroke represents a different historical state whether painting, using the healing brush, or cloning, for example, so fifty isn't as much as it seems. You may tell Photoshop to recall more historical states (Edit-Preferences-Performance), but keep in mind that doing so will slow down Photoshop's performance (conversely, if you are running Photoshop on an older or slower machine you might want to decrease the number of history states to help improve performance). Another reason snapshots may be beneficial is that they enable you to undo to a point farther back in history than your history panel would normally allow.

It's vital to remember that snapshots and history states (and hence the ability to undo) are preserved in Photoshop's working memory rather than being saved with the file. You lose those history states and can no longer reverse past modifications after you close a picture and/or shut Photoshop. This emphasizes the importance of the non-destructive strategies we'll discuss later in the text!

History Brush

The History Brush is a tool that allows you to undo changes to a specific area of your picture. If you alter the brightness of your picture and like the impact on the majority of it but not the sky, you may utilize the History Brush to undo just the sky area of your image.

- To utilize the History Brush, first choose how far back in your change history you wish to travel. In the Historical Window, there is a box to the left of each history state. A brush symbol will show when you click next to the past state you wish to return to.

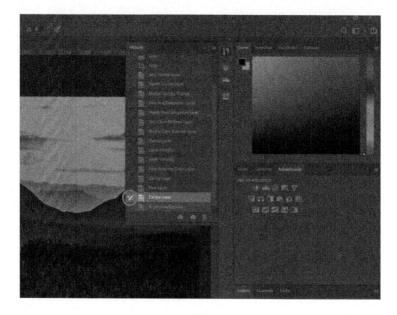

- Then, from the Tool Panel, pick the history brush tool and paint over the section of the picture you wish to undo. You can change the size, flow, opacity, hardness, and blending mode of the History Brush since it's a brush tool.

Non-Destructive Editing

The fact that undo (and the History Panel) is a liner is its largest constraint. You're taking a step back in time as a result of the alterations you've made. If you make a mistake and don't discover it until later, you'll have to undo everything that came before it in order to correct it. This may vary from somewhat unpleasant to incredibly aggravating and time-consuming, depending on when you recognize your error or realize you need to modify anything. And that presupposes you catch your error before closing your picture or shutting off Photoshop, since you can't reverse anything after you leave the session you're working on.

This is where the concept of non-destructive labor comes into play. Making modifications directly to a picture is referred to as destructive work since the alterations are permanent. Making modifications to a picture that may be undone or adjusted later is known as non-destructive editing. It is possible to work with layers and adjustment layers in such a manner that undo/redo and making adjustments is a breeze. And, unlike in the past, you can save your picture with the layers intact, allowing you to make those adjustments even after closing and reopening the image. If you're not sure what layers are or how they function in Photoshop, you should read Spencer's explanation of layers, adjustment layers, and layer masking, since these are the foundations of non-destructive editing.

Layers

Any time you make significant modifications to a picture, you should do it on a new layer. You should utilize layers sparingly since they increase file size and, as a consequence, may slow down Photoshop on a slower system. Use a new layer if you're making modifications that would take more than a minute or two to recreate if you had to do them all over again. When you isolate modifications to their own layer, you may edit, lower opacity, and even remove the layer (basically undoing those changes) without impacting any other adjustments you've made to the picture.

When you open a picture in Photoshop, the first thing you should do is duplicate the background layer. This assures that you are working on a duplicate of the picture and that you can always return to the original. However, you don't want to make all of your adjustments to the same duplicate layer. If you're cloning or using the healing brush or patch tools, create a new layer so you can simply undo, redo, or mask your changes.

In the Layers panel, there is an eye symbol next to each layer. The layer will become invisible if you click this symbol. Toggling the visibility of a layer enables you to see the results of the changes you've made without having to choose a state permanently (similar to the "Toggle Last State" Command). If you're not sure about a change, hide the layer and come back to it later, while toggling the last state forces you to make a choice right now. Layer visibility enables you to view all of the modifications that are part of that layer, while the undo toggle simply shows you the latest change you made.

Adjustment Layers

All of the tools in the Picture-Adjustments Menu may be used as adjustment layers when making changes to your image. When you use the Picture-Adjustments Menu to make a modification, it is applied straight to your image.

You can perform the exact same modification but on a different layer if you use adjustment layers (if the Adjustment Layer Panel isn't already visible, pick it from the Window Menu). Adjustment layers enable you to add layer masks, modify the opacity, eliminate an adjustment entirely, or go back and make adjustments to it at any time, even after you've moved on to another part of the picture.

Chapter 8

How to Crop a Photo

Cropping a picture reduces the amount of pixels by removing pixels from the surrounding region. Cropping a picture in Adobe Photoshop is done with the Crop tool or the Crop command.

To use the Crop tool to crop a picture, follow these steps:

1. From the Tool Panel, select the **Crop tool** or click C.

2. Move the mouse to a location on the picture that will be a border of the cropped image and left-click the mouse.

3. Move the cursor diagonally while holding down the left mouse button.

4. Let go of the left mouse button. A box with indicated corners will emerge over the picture, showing the region that will be saved. This box may be resized, rotated, and moved around.

    •   To reposition the crop box Move the cursor entirely within the chosen area, hold down the left mouse button, and drag the box while holding down the left mouse button.

- Move the pointer to one of the border markers, press the left mouse button, then drag the marker to modify the size of the chosen area. The size of the box will be proportionately altered if the cursor is moved while pressing **Shift.**

- Move the mouse to one of the corner markers and drag the cursor to rotate the crop box.

- To crop the picture, hit **ENTER** (or RETURN on a Mac) or the checkbox button in the Options Panel.
- Press ESC on your keyboard to dismiss the crop box without cropping the picture.

Follow these instructions to crop a picture using the Crop command from the Photoshop menu:

1. From the Tool Panel, select the Rectangular mar-quee tool.
2. Using the picture Selection Tools in Adobe Photoshop, choose a rectangle region.
3. From the Image menu, choose **Crop.**

How to Flip and Rotate Photos

The Picture - Rotate Canvas submenu in Adobe Photoshop can be used to rotate an image.

The following commands can be used:

- 180° – the picture is rotated by 180 degrees.
- 90° CW turns the picture clockwise by 90 degrees.
- 90° CCW – spins the picture anticlockwise by 90 degrees.
- Arbitrary – this command spins the picture in any direction. For this reason:

The process:

1. From the menu, pick the command;
2. Enter the degree value of the rotation angle;
3. Select the rotation's direction (clockwise or anti-clockwise);

4. Click the **OK button**.

The following instructions from the menu Image – Rotate Canvas in Adobe Photoshop may be used to flip an image:

- **Horizontal Flip** – mirrors the picture with relation to the standing axis, i.e. swaps the left and right halves of the image;
- **Flip Vertical** – flips the picture upside down by mirroring it along the horizontal axis.

How to Change the Size of an Image

Do you have a lot of excellent images that you'd want to print but you are not satisfied with their sizes? Simply follow the instructions.

Follow these procedures in Adobe Photoshop to adjust the picture size for printing:

1. From Adobe Photoshop's Image menu, choose the **Image Size command**.

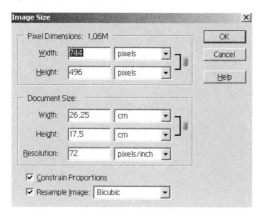

2. To retain the picture dimensions, tick the option **Constrain Proportions**.

3. If you wish to keep the picture resolution the same, click the option Resample Image.

4. Choose from Nearest Neighbour, Bilinear, and Bicubic interpolation methods. The Bicubic technique of interpolation is recommended.

5. Select units in the group Document Size and add new values in the Width and Height boxes. The resolution will vary if the checkbox Resample Image is not selected.

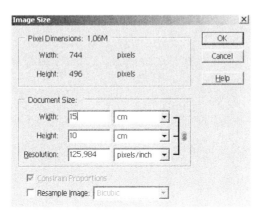

6. Finally, hit the **OK button**.

Chapter 9

How to Add Text

Adding text to your photos allows you to be creative – or to provide guidance or explanation to a design.

Adding Text

Here's how:

- When adding text to an image, you have the option of using horizontal text (text that runs across the image) or vertical text (text that runs from top to bottom).

- The Text tool is used to add text. It's on the Tools panel.

By default, the Horizontal Text tool is visible.

- To utilize the Vertical Text tool, go to the Tool Options panel and choose Vertical Text from the list.

- For the time being, let's use the Horizontal Text tool.
- To add a line of text to your picture, first click where you want the text to appear in the image.
- A flickering cursor will appear, along with a box with a green checkmark and a red circle.

- Just begin typing. The text will be displayed on top of your picture.

- When you've completed typing and formatting the text, click the green checkmark. Formatting will be discussed later in this essay.
- When you add text to a picture, it is placed on a separate layer.

Text Boxes: How to Make Them

You may also type text into a text box. Simply drag a rectangle across the screen in the location where you want the paragraph to go to create a paragraph of text. This will result in the creation of a text box.

- To begin typing, just click within the text area.
- When you've completed inserting and formatting content, click the green checkmark.

How to Format Text

Going to the Tool Options panel and utilizing the usual formatting tools available there is all it takes to format text.

Look at the Horizontal Text Tool Options menu and you have the option of changing the font type.

- You may also modify the font size or change the font style.

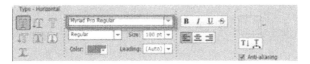

- To change the font color, go to the **C**olor **dropdown menu**.

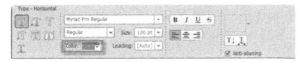

- To change the leading, choose it from the Leading dropdown list.

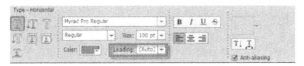

- Make the text stand out by bolding, italicizing, or underlining it. Strikethrough text is also an option.

- Text may also be aligned to the left, center, or right.

- Toggle the text orientation by clicking the first button below. This function changes horizontal to vertical text and vice versa. To distort text, use the second button.

- Set your settings in the Tool Options window, including font, color, and size. In the settings box, you may also twist text and create various effects.

- Simply hold down your mouse button and drag it over the text that appears on your picture to format it. As seen below, this picks the text.

- Apply whatever text formatting you desire, then click the green checkmark (as seen above) when you're done.

Chapter 10

How to Select and Move Text

If you add text to a picture, you may wish to transfer it to a different location. Keep in mind that your text is a separate layer. As a result, we'll shift the layer in order to relocate the text.

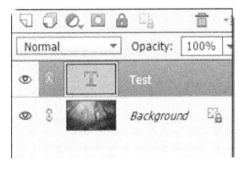

- To move a layer, first pick it in the Layers panel, then go to the Tools panel and choose the **Move tool**.

- In the Layers panel, you can see the text layer.

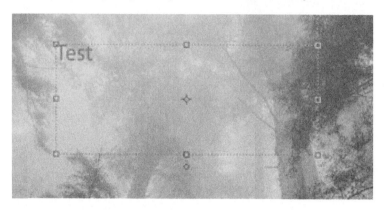

How to Use the Text on Custom Path Tool to Add Text to a Path

Along the custom path, you may draw and add text. Here's how:

- Select the **Text on Custom Path** tool from the toolbox. Press **Option** and then click the current text tool to swiftly change it.
- Over the picture, draw a custom path. From the tool options bar, you may commit/cancel the drawn route to redraw it.

- In the tool options box, click **Modify** to revise or redraw the route. To change the route, use the nodes that appear on it.

- After you've finished drawing a route, you may add text by clicking anywhere along it with your mouse. Modify the text in the same manner you would regular text.

- After you've finished typing, click **Commit**.

How to Add Custom Shapes

First of all, you will need to download the custom shapes you want to add from a trusted website.

Once downloaded, continue by following the steps below:

- Go to the location where you stored the file. The file containing the shapes usually has a .zip extension.

- Because this isn't a Photoshop-compatible file, you'll need to unzip or extract it.

- If you have an app to unzip the file, it should display in the list of choices when you right-click the file name. (I use 7-Zip for this.)

- Unzip is the option here. The Custom Shape file (.csh) will be saved in the same folder.

Chapter 11

How to Add Shapes to Photoshop Elements 2022

Now you must copy and paste the .csh file into the Custom Shapes folder in Photoshop Element. What happened to that folder? It's hidden deep in your C drive, to be sure. Here's how to get there:

- Open Windows File Explorer if you're using Windows. Choose C:Program Files (x86) if you have a 64-bit machine, then **Adobe > Photoshop Elements 2022 > Presets > Custom Shapes**.

- Go to **Adobe Photoshop Elements 2022 > Support files > Presets > Custom Shapes** on a Mac. [The Support files folder may or may not be present. If not, just search for Presets].

- You may open Photoshop after copying and pasting the .csh file into the Custom Shapes folder. If you already have Photoshop Elements open, shut it and reopen it (after saving your work).

- Now open a file, choose your **Custom Shape Tool** from the toolbar, and open the dropdown menu next to the shape icon, followed by the dropdown menu with the names list.

The name of the custom shape file you just copied and pasted should appear. Select one of the new forms by clicking on that name.

How to Sharpen Images

The following are working tips to sharpen images on Photoshop Elements 2022:

1. Get rid of blemishes

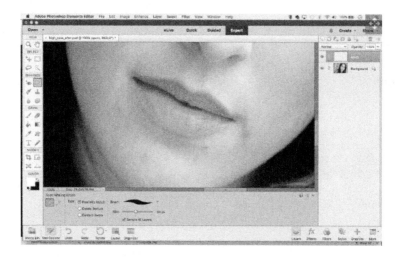

Open high pass before .jpg in a new window. To enter Expert Mode, click the **'Expert'** button at the top. Click the New Layer button in the Layers window. To erase markings, choose the Spot Healing Brush tool from the toolbar, check the 'Sample All Layers' option in the tool preferences, and then paint over them.

2. Use high pass

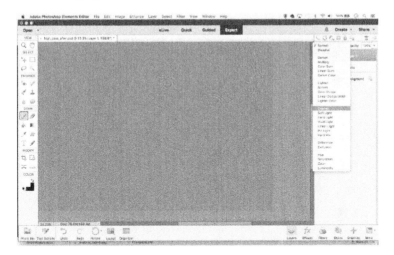

To combine the layers, press Cmd/Ctrl+Shift+Alt+E. Select Filter>Other>High Pass from the Filter menu. The ideal intensity varies depending on the picture and quality, but it should start at approximately 8. Select OK. Change the blending mode in the Layers window from Normal to Overlay. This has the effect of sharpening the image.

3. Make the skin soft

To convert the effect from sharpening to softening, use Cmd/Ctrl+I to invert the layer. In the Layers panel, click the Add Mask icon, then Cmd/Ctrl+I to invert the mask to black. Select the Brush tool, set the color to white, and paint over the skin to see the softening effect.

4. Sharpen the lashes

To create a new merged layer, press Cmd/Ctrl+Shift+Alt+E. Select Filter>Other>High Pass from the Filter menu. We'll use the filter for a sharpening effect this time, so use a smaller amount; try 2-3. Change the layer's blending mode to Overlay, then create a layer mask, as previously.

5. Selectively sharpen

When it comes to portraiture, it's preferable to apply sharpness to specific parts rather than the full face. To hide the effect, press Cmd/Ctrl+I to invert the layer mask to black. To expose the sharpness, use the Brush tool to paint white over the eyes, lashes, and lips.

6. Dodge and Burn

To modify the sharpening intensity, use the Layer Opacity control. Finally, you have to burn the face by dodging and burning it. In the Layers panel, alt-click the New Layer icon. Check the 'Fill with...' box and choose Mode: Overlay. Paint white to lighten regions and black to darken them using the Brush tool.

How to Edit Raw Files in Photoshop Elements 2022

Modern digital cameras offer a number of benefits over film, the most important of which being the ability to shoot Raw files, which include a wealth of exposure data. This provides a safety net in case your exposure or white balance is off, as well as the ability to fine-tune the photographs to your liking.

Raw isn't an abbreviation; it refers to the raw data that comes directly from the camera's sensor. Each camera manufacturer's raw file format, such as, is unique. On most Canon cameras, CR2 files are used, or. Nikons use NEF files. They are frequently five to ten times bigger than JPEGs, depending on the body, therefore memory cards will fill up considerably faster.

However, it's definitely worth the additional cost to receive the raw data, which allows you to fix white balance, tweak exposure, and make a slew of other useful modifications that are considerably more difficult to do with a compressed JPEG file. When you capture a JPEG, the colors, contrast, and other factors are 'baked in,' and most of the extra data is thrown away, but Raw files give you the freedom to polish them up precisely as you want.

To use Photoshop Elements 2022, just open a Raw file that you wish to edit and drag it into the program. It will then be immediately transferred to a simplified version of Adobe Camera Raw, where we can make some critical modifications to enhance the image and fully use the raw data.

1. Make a crop and a straightening

It's advisable to use the Crop Tool to achieve the composition you want before making any substantial modifications. This means you won't waste time tweaking pixels that won't appear in the final product, and you can even correct the horizon while you're doing it.

2. Make a white balance adjustment

When dealing with a JPEG, adjusting white balance may be difficult, but since Raws include so much more exposure information, it's simple to alter using the Temperature slider to make the image colder or warmer. You may also choose one of the presets from the drop-down menu.

3. Adjust the exposure to perfection

Adjusting the exposure is another difficult task with JPEGs. But that's not an issue with Raw files, because with all that additional info, you can normally make your photos at least two stops brighter or darker without sacrificing image quality.

4. Increase the contrast

Using the Highlights, Shadows, Whites, and Blacks sliders, we can finally create the precise contrast we desire in the scenario. To increase the dynamic range of the scene, drag Shadows and Whites to the right and Highlights and Blacks to the left.

5. Give the hues a little kick

Drag the Vibrance and Saturation sliders to the right to make the colors in your photo more vibrant, or to the left to remove color. Because Vibrance boosts the least saturated colors first, it's a little less obvious than the Saturation slider.

6. Make your shots more precise

Set the Sharpening Amount to 50 on the Detail panel. Holding the Alt key, adjust the Masking slider until only the sections you want to sharpen are visible in white (a value of 80 or 90 on our photo), then apply Noise Reduction if necessary, then select **Open Image**.

Chapter 12

How to Use Selective Color to Make Your Images Stand Out

Here are the processes to take to make your images stand out while using selective color:

1. Make your picture less saturated

In Photoshop Elements 2022, open your picture and go to the Layers panel (Window>Layers). Now choose Hue/Saturation from the Create new adjustment layer menu. Set the Saturation slider to -100 in the new panel to drain all the color.

2. Get the Brush Tool ready

To paint color back into the picture, choose the Brush Tool from the Toolbox and click it to activate it. Set the Opacity to 70% under Tool Options, then click on Brush Settings and change the Hardness to 80%. Now use the sliders or the square bracket keys to resize your brush.

3. Begin working on the Layer Mask

To make your brush black, click on the layer mask of your hue/saturation layer to make it active, then press D followed by X. Press **Ctrl (PC) or CMD (Mac)** plus the + key a few times to zoom in, then paint over your subject to restore the bright color.

4. Use the preview overlay to your advantage

To use the preview overlay, use the key, which turns any places you've painted on your layer mask bright red, making it easy to notice whether you've missed or overpainted anything. By continuously tapping the key, you can turn it on or off.

5. To cover the effect, repaint it

If you accidently paint over a region you don't want to color pop, just press X on your computer to switch to a white foreground color and brush over it to desaturate it. To continue working, press X once again for a white foreground color.

6. Increase the contrast

We're going to improve the contrast in your photo to give it one last dramatic push. Return to the Levels panel and click the **Create new adjustment layer button**, then choose **Levels** from the drop-down menu. Drag the Blacks and Whites sliders inwards in the Levels panel.

Tips and Tricks for Photo Editing

Photoshop Elements from Adobe may seem to be nothing more than a low-cost alternative to Photoshop, but it's more than that. Photoshop is a professional graphics program (not merely an image editor) with capabilities and features that most photographers would never use.

With a few exceptions (most notably Curves and Layer Masks), Elements shares the most of Photoshop's photo-editing features. It also includes Adobe's superb picture cataloguing application, Organizer.

1. Control color settings

Choose how Elements manages the working color space by going to **Edit > Color Settings**. Select **"Always optimize colors."** for ordinary onscreen viewing or **"Always optimize for printing"** to utilize the AdobeRGB color space's expanded gamut. Alternatively, for ad-hoc switching, choose **"Allow me to choose."**

2. Keep an eye on your step

You may move backwards through the changes you've made by continuously hitting the [Ctrl] + [Z] key combination when editing photos, then forward again by pressing [Ctrl] + [Y].

3. Make your choices as quickly as possible

The process of lassoing and identifying portions of a picture may be time-consuming. The primary tool palette's Quick Selection tool is a super-fast alternative that works well.

4. Improve the image's sharpness

Use the Unsharp Mask tool to sharpen a whole picture, or use the Quick Selection tool to pre-define the region to be sharpened first (such as the eyes in a portrait).

5. Change the mode to automatic

Enhancing your photos doesn't have to be a time-consuming or difficult task. With a single mouse click, you may perform a completely automated Smart Fix when you go to the Quick Edit workspace. Alternatively, use a sliding scale to choose the amount of fixing.

6. Go back in time

Switching to imperial ruler measures in the Preferences dialog's Units & Rulers section is useful for dealing with typical picture print sizes like 6 x 4-inch.

7. Make your photos as big as possible

Elements does an excellent job at enlarging photos that are quite modest. Enter the new dimensions in Image > Resize > Image Size, then click Resample Image and pick Bicubic

Smoother. Click Constrain Proportions as well.

8. Make your gloomy sky blue

Smart Brushes in Photoshop Elements 2022 apply a layer mask selection in real time as well as an effect when you paint over portions of a picture. The Blue Skies option greatly enhances British summers!

9. Conserve disk space

If you utilize a lot of layers in Photoshop, the file size might quickly balloon. Use the Flatten Image option to reduce final photos to a single layer to conserve disk space.

10. Use monochrome to create a mood

The Enhance pulldown menu has a fantastic Black & White conversion tool, with settings including Portraits, Scenic Landscapes, and Infrared Effect.

Conclusion

From this guide, it is clear that the new Adobe Photoshop Elements 2022 is the perfect editing tool for photographers, online bloggers, web designers, and so much more. It comes with a whole lot of new features including automated editing, create and share, organization and so much more.

Furthermore, this guide also covers the several ways to create mind-blowing and build on stunning images to make them even much more appealing to viewers. Simply get this guide to begin or strengthen your photo-editing skills.